CLARENCE JOSEPH RIVERS
REFLECTIONS

DESIGNER: WILLIAM SCHICKEL & ASSOCIATES ● PUBLISHER: HERDER AND HERDER   NEW YORK

Library of Congress Catalog Number: 77-122328
© 1970 by Clarence Joseph Rivers
Manufactured in the United States
Published by Herder and Herder
232 Madison Avenue, New York 10016

CONTENTS

INTRODUCTION

Living in a time of rapid change is difficult for the average man. Things happen to him so quickly that he has little time to think before responding. The quick pace of his life dawns on him when he goes to bed tired, wanting to sleep, but unable to slow down.

In an effort to get a hold on life, some men stand fixed, refusing to change. They find a comfortable posture, and become skeptical of anything beyond the boundaries of the little world they have created for themselves. They find little value in anything outside of what is familiar.

Other men, on the other hand, respond to rapid change by losing all deep roots. They seem to live for another world, inspired by their political or religious ideals. They excuse their inability to cope with life by placing their hopes in some never-never land.

Both of these ways through life alienate men from one another. Ultimately, such paths even alienate a man from himself. He loses his ability to articulate the value of life, to express to someone else what life means to him, to find within himself the strength to be the master of his destiny. He not only wonders about how he can be himself; he is even uncertain about who he is. Constantly he confronts the question: How can I live as a man of the times without becoming one of time's victims?

REFLECTIONS is a collection of essays and homilies in which I have tried to articulate some of my experience in the world today. I offer them not as **the** way through uncertainty and change, but in the hope that the reader may find here some balance as he walks the tightrope of our times.

Clarence Jos. Rivers

A BRIEF THEOLOGY OF PRAGMATISM

I'm infuriated by that red, white and blue bumper-sticker that says, "America—Love it or leave it." It suggests that love is not critical, does not face up to the truth. So I much prefer another sticker which did not enjoy the slick chrome of so many bumpers: "America — Fix it or forget it." We who love America cannot be satisfied with her as she is, or one day her imperfections will be her undoing. If we allow America to become a harbor of racism, of poverty in the midst of plenty, we cannot claim to love her.

I came to know this kind of love for one's country after having lived in Europe. (I did not leave America following the advice of the "love it or leave it" sticker. I went to Europe to study the history of Christian ritual.) My experience abroad taught me the value of my American heritage. I came to see through the myth which contrasts the rich American barbarian to the highly cultured, though technologically improverished European. America isn't really any better or any worse, as a whole, than any other country.

I'd be hard pressed to know where to go if I took the advice of that sticker. This isn't the same as saying we are as good as we ought to be or even as good as we could be. But if we are to appreciate our worth, we must cast off our inferiority complex. Like her Negro sons, who are coming to know that "Black is Beautiful," all Americans must come to a sense of their dignity as a people and as a nation. If we don't believe that we can better our nation, we won't. We are a great country, a people whose deepest resources are still to be tapped. If we can believe this of ourselves without simply seeking to satisfy our ego, which is so badly bruised these days, we can come again to see that red, white and blue is beautiful, too.

America has not accomplished her place in the world simply by holding tenaciously to precious ideals. Somehow in America people are able to make ideals work, often without being able to clearly articulate why something ought to be done, or why something should happen. Americans just seem to be able to do things that large numbers of people simply talk about. Americans don't operate by creating some ideal state in the mind. They operate with the stuff of statehood—with the fire of conflict and debate, with a plurality of beliefs, with working out the things that need to be done to form a great nation. Americans are practical idealists. **America has been able to do what she has done specifically because she could not be idealistic in a monomaniacal way.** There are too many people with conflicting ideals living in America for us to allow any one ideal to become a maniacal fixation.

Some are now crying for a real political choice, for third and fourth parties. Such aspirations imply that the major parties are such a mixture of conservatives and liberals that there is no real difference between the programs they devise, and so the parties give the voter no real choice. But I don't believe this is entirely so. I would much prefer selecting between two hybrids, rather than two polarized **inbred** programs. The hybrid party can offer a cross-fertilization of liberal and conservative positions, and possibly provide a combination of the strengths of each, minimizing the effects of the weaknesses of each.

Ideals are not something that one imposes on reality from the outside. They arise from what needs to be done. To be true to an ideal is to recognize the truth of reality. So does God, whom we sometimes describe as the ultimate truth, exist not outside reality but as the root and ground of all being. Therefore one cannot enjoy a genuine faith by following an abstract God. One meets God in the everyday realities.

Every effort to follow abstract ideals slavishly is sure to fail. Even in the history of literature this is evident. Those writers of the neo-classic period who tried to use the rules of Aristotle as if they were recipes did not produce great art. These writers were not dealing with the realities of life as did, for instance, William Shakespeare. Shakespeare could never have achieved his powerful moments in drama had he not dealt with life's realities and allowed his dramatic form to flow from these realities.

We are not given a definition of man and then asked to live up to it. We are given our manhood and asked to live up to whatever being a man demands. Similarly, the person who has faith does not impose his belief on life. He comes to believe because faith is what life asks of him.

A person can practice his faith by regular church attendance, but this can become an abstract faith. Some would identify loss of faith with the decline in attendance at worship services. This decline should concern us, but more important to me is the lifelessness of the people who say they believe. It strikes me that the decline in traditional practices of faith is consistent with the American personality I have been describing. The American is a practical man, one who cannot live according to abstract ideals. He is finding the church-going kind of faith an abstract ideal, and so he is finding it meaningless. But this does not mean he is losing his faith. He may be discovering faith anew by discovering a practical belief in life, the will to experiment, and to live in uncertainty while trying an unknown. This is the American way.

I am reminded of a conversation with a French Jesuit on the proposed "experiments" which would move the Jesuit houses of study onto university campuses. He said he knew American Jesuits who had already decided to move, so he had asked one how he could be sure that the new program would work. The American replied that they would try it and see whether it would work. In contrast, the French Jesuit said that in France they had called a meeting to explore the possibilities and were given a 500-page study of the proposal; but no action was foreseen (in spite of the 500-page study) until the proposal was thought out for another five to ten years.

The ecumenical movement is another instance of the American existential approach to life proving more fruitful than the usual European academic, analytical approach. At the grass roots level there is more American ecumenism (much of which preceded even official attempts) simply because Americans do more practical living together than Europeans.

The liturgical movement in the United States is one more example of an expression of the American way. Nothing in Europe equals our grass-roots Liturgical Conference. Although its roots are European, the main thrust of the American movement is more pastoral than any European counterpart. The American movement is characteristically trying to be faithful to the biblical injunctions to make righteous social living a prime prerequisite to any act of worship. In contrast, liturgy in Europe is predominantly a scholarly pursuit. I am reminded of an eminent European theologian who told me that he saw no immediate connection between liturgical and social concerns.

The power of the concrete as opposed to the abstract can be seen in another way. It is experience, truth incarnate, truth in operation, rather than abstract argument, which convinces and converts. Many traditionalists have been converted to "the new liturgy" by participating in an effective new liturgical style. Few, if any, have been converted by hearing good reasons for having liturgy renewed.

To do what works seems to me to be the way of the artist; not only of the artist of paint, stone, and wood, but of the artist of life, of the person who is able to live creatively.

I would suggest that "what works" is the guide for "what one ought to do." In other words, one is moral when one is practical. Consider how at one time the Church forbade usury, and how she now is a holder of no few stocks. This change came about after people of the world made a practical decision to collect interest on money, having seen that this practice was important to the economic development of the world. The Church is no less moral because she changed her position. On the contrary, from the practical decision of the people, the Church came to know a new morality. Pragmatism is not to be dismissed as morally suspect. Morality often comes from pragmatism at work.

St. John spoke as a pragmatist when he said that only a practical, a doing

13

love is a valid love. "Let us love not merely in words but let our love be something real and active."

If what I have said here isn't clear, let me say it all again very briefly. The way in which one lives up to an ideal is by being practical. There is, as I see it, no contradiction between the ideal and the practical.

LAW AND LOVE

Some time ago I saw a cartoon in which a cave man with a huge club on his shoulder was at the controls of a nuclear-powered rocket. An inscription on the rocket read "brand new technology." Another inscription on the club read "same old morality." What the cartoon said so forcefully, John Kennedy spelled out a little more in detail when he said, "Unless man can match his strides in technology and weaponry with equal strides in social and political development, man's great strength, like that of the dinosaur, will become incapable of proper control, and man, like the dinosaur, will vanish from the face of the earth." The rate of technological progress is accelerating, but morality lags far behind.

How sophisticated we think we are. We look with amazement and disdain at the barbarisms of the Roman Empire and its gladitorial games; and we are horrified by the stupidity of the Middle Ages with its crusades and witch hunts and trials by combat. We are far removed from the **lex talionis** that demanded an eye for an eye and a tooth for a tooth. But in the very act of turning up our collective nose at the barbarisms of old, we remove our sights from the barbarisms of the present which should have been in our line of vision.

Perhaps we have abolished the gladitorial arena. But wait a minute; have we? Don't we still have the boxing ring and the bullring, and don't we feel cheated if blood isn't drawn, or if the contest is over too quickly — that is, before we get our money's worth of seeing one man skillfully impose brutal punishment on another man or an animal? We are fascinated by the sight of blood being spilled.

Oh, I know that we tend to justify all this by saying we admire the fighters' skill, nothing more; but our lie is found out when we fail to patronize college boxing and wrestling where the possibility of injury is kept at a minimum. Such is uninteresting.

Scoff as we will at the men of earlier times for attempting to settle disputes by killing one another in a trial of arms, are we not equally (on all sides of our conflicts) contending that "Might makes Right"? We have not yet learned to settle disputes by rational discourse rather than by force and violence.

Scoff as we will at primitive tribes that allowed an eye for an eye and a tooth for a tooth, do we not, through our penal institutions, seek our revenge? We do not want to reclaim the criminal so much as we want to **make him pay,** even with his life at times—especially if he has taken a life. No matter how you read it, we have not come very far morally.

Now the Church, among her other functions, exists to stimulate moral progress in society. But we find even the Church compromising her duty —on the grounds of not expecting people to live up to the ideal. It would be impractical to expect so much. But there is no other way than to try to live up to the ideal. That is the only practical way to live.

The practical life, which is also ideal, is the life of love. Love is ideal in that it is a free and generous giving based not on what the other deserves (justice) but rather on the giver's willingness to share his goods freely with another, especially in light of the other's need. This selfless giving is the source of all creation. God made the world in a completely free act of generosity. Nothing compelled God to share his existence, except his own impulse to do so. Certainly it was not strict legal justice that moved God to create. Rather God freely gave of himself.

Love freely given is also a prerequisite for family life. It is the married couple's selfless love which gives birth to children. Even if children grow up a disappointment to their parents, they are still loved—in spite of what they might deserve in justice.

And now, more and more, states and federations of states are groping blindly for a society based on love. This search does not follow abstract ideals. It is forced upon man out of the need to survive. In a nuclear age we have come to see how giving an enemy his just deserts could destroy society. We have come to see that we must refrain from indiscriminate force directed against an unfriendly nation—not because they deserve our restraint, but because the use of such force will return like a ghost to haunt us.

In our overpopulated and underdeveloped world—yet a world so closely knit by progress in methods of transportation and communication—we are forced to realize that a man needs to be fed and educated, not because he has earned the right, but because he is a man.

Every day it becomes clearer that the concept of a society built on narrow legal justice is inadequate for the well-being of the world. At last the moral injunction of the idealist prophets can be preached as a practical matter: we must love or we will perish.

RELIGIOUS SCHIZOPHRENIA

When someone says, "That's the way the ball bounces" or "That's the way the cookie crumbles," there are few of us so literal-minded as to wonder, "What ball?" or "What cookie?" We know without explanation that the kind of language which best reveals the truth of life is indirect, poetic, metaphorical.

It has indeed been a long time since men have considered the darkness of night to be a source of evil, and the light of day a source of good. Today we know that many good things come from darkness—and that too much light is not always a good thing. Although we still preserve within our language the metaphors which imply that darkness is evil and that light is good, we do not usually take metaphors literally, **unless** the metaphor happens to be found in Scripture; then, for some reason, we become quite literal-minded.

We read in Peter's epistle the admonition to "abstain from the passions of the flesh that wage war against the soul," and we conclude in the most simple-minded fashion that the flesh is the enemy of the soul. Nothing could be further from the intention of the sacred writers. They use metaphorical language simply to express the contest between good and evil that goes on within us. In fact, no clear distinction between body and soul can be found in the Bible. When the Jewish writers spoke of the soul, they meant (in our terms) the whole human person.

If we understand the metaphorical usage of certain words and passages of the New and Old Testaments, we will find no scriptural justification for our puritanical suspicions about the World and the Flesh of Man, no justification for our sometimes neurotic fear of the sensual. We need look no farther than St. Peter's epistle to see that the Christian is meant to respect and embrace the world: "Be subject," says Peter, "to every human institution . . . for such is the will of God."

20

Open your Bible and read the Canticle of Canticles (or the Song of Solomon), a poetic work expressing the highly sensual-sexual relationship between a man and a woman. (No mention of God or the angels or "things spiritual"; but his shape and her shape, and how sweet they are.) Read this acknowledged Holy Book and know that neither Christian nor Jew need apologize for using the sensual or sexual to give concrete expression to what we have thought of as the transcendent love between God and his people.

I say all this in the context of using "secular" or "popular" or "folk" or "jazz" music in the liturgy. I often hear the objection that these musics have no place in the liturgy because they are associated with "worldly concerns" or because they are associated with the sensual and even the sexual. But, I say, if they have no place in the liturgy, then **The Canticle of Canticles** has no place in the Bible.

We actually worry about using strong rhythms in church music, ignorant of the fact that the psalms themselves are so called because they were considered "hand-clapping songs."

I have chosen "The Brotherhood of Man" as the title for one of my liturgical compositions because brotherhood is a basic prerequisite for any act of worship in the Jewish and Christian traditions. The constant message of the prophets was that God rejected religious rites divorced from a social life of active concern for one's brother in need. And Christ himself reminded us that if we come to the altar and there remember that anything separates us from our brothers, we should go first to be reconciled to our brothers, and only then return to the altar.

Music really ought to be a bridge of unity and understanding between brothers of different cultures. Oddly enough, however, music at present often puts us in danger of violating the precept of brotherhood. In an attempt to satisfy what seems to be the divergent needs of classicists, folkists, and jazzists, we are in effect setting up cultural apartheid. More and more we are saying, for example, "Let those who want folk music have their own liturgy," or "Let teenagers have their own liturgy." If we are implying that various cultural groups cannot worship together, I agree that under some circumstances separation may be an immediate necessity. But I cannot agree that it can ever be a long-range ideal goal.

The Churches have put themselves on the side of racial and social integration, considering it a moral imperative. Yet the sin of cultural segregation and intolerance is permitted to exist. The logical question is whether lovers of the popular, the classical, the folk, the jazz, can endure one another's tastes, can love and associate with one another. Should we not pass up the temptation to solve cultural tensions by a facile recourse to cultural apartheid? If the command to love can require that I be willing to be present to my neighbor of a different color or nationality, can it not also require that I be willing to be present to my neighbor of a different cultural background?

I believe that cultural integration is as much a moral imperative as racial integration. Separate but equal facilities are neither possible nor desirable. And if an integrated cultural situation is not immediately comfortable, if it requires a painful process, we ought to remember that love will always require some sacrifice.

But while cultural integration will require sacrifice, the positive benefits will be much greater than the initial cost. At present, the musical climate in most churches is terribly monotonous. With cultural integration, we will enjoy a variety of music. The interplay of these various forms previously (and needlessly) considered incompatible will stimulate originality.

In music, as in the divorce courts, incompatibility is frequently revealed to be intolerance; and intolerance should be intolerable in churches that claim to be based on love. With the spirit of generosity and of tolerance toward one another, we can in all things make the music of God's peace.

SMILE!

In both Advent and Lent the Church reminds us with somber violet and a call to repentance that redemption in this world is incomplete. But the Church is not content to let us remember the sorrow of unredemption without at the same time reminding us that Christ our hope is near, and for that reason we should be able to rejoice. This is the meaning of the rose vestments in the middle of Advent and Lent. We are not without hope even when we are desperate. Christ is near. In the words of St. Paul quoted in the Advent liturgy, "Never cease to be joyful in the Lord; again I say it, be joyful. Let all men feel the warmth of your heart."

Nevertheless, Christians are not generally known for their joy in the Lord. In the average mind, whether Christian or not, sorrow and glumness and downcast eyes and joyless faces are the hallmarks of holiness. Sadness is considered more reverent than laughter; for although one may cry in church without being reprimanded, no one dares laugh. In all the years that I have been giving communion to the faithful, seldom have I seen anyone smile. There have been many downcast eyes and mournful looks, and sometimes tears, but seldom a smile.

Taken to its logical conclusion, our idea of reverence becomes something of a heresy: despair and gloom are more God-like than hope and joy. This kind of "witness" is a disservice to the faith. Something is wrong, dreadfully wrong, with the way that religion manifests itself in our lives. My prayer every Gaudete and Laetare Sunday is that some day soon these rituals of joy will no longer be merely rituals, but dynamic parts of our real lives. We are supposed to be heralds and bearers of the Good News to the world. But God help us—if we continue to look as we have looked, no one will believe that we have any good news at all. For heaven's sake, smile!

BLACK-WHITE SCHIZOPHRENIA

"Integration" was well on its way to becoming a sacred word, one that was due the unquestioning reverence traditionally reserved for "motherhood," "patriotism," and "religion." But then some black Americans, in whose behalf this blessing had been invoked, all of a sudden, it seemed, began saying that they were no longer interested in integration. They became quite angry at the supposition that integration was an ideal state, to be desired by the black man.

Then black men who repudiated integration came to be called "separatists." (You certainly couldn't call a black man a "segregationist," could you?) And now certain of the avant-garde white liberals, almost with drill-team precision, made an about-face, dropped their integrationist rhetoric and picked up the separatist rhetoric, which they repeated uncritically with a kind of fundamentalist literalism. At the same time certain black men like myself, having for so long preached the immorality of segregation, rushed at once to point out that segregation under some other name was still immoral; and moreover, that ethnic isolationism in the latter half of the twentieth century A.D. was a primitive and impractical tribal superstition.

But neither my own immediate recourse to moralizing nor the uncritical about-face of the liberal was an appropriate response to the threat of black separatism. The latter was inappropriate because it supposed that black men really did want to live separately. The former was inappropriate because it supposed that the integration that we had been preaching was truly opposed to the new separatism. Such was not the case. **The new call for separatism was very much in accord with the ideals of integration.**

In spite of the fact that separatist statements seemed uncompromising, those statements were nonetheless conditional. What black men were saying was that **superficial** integration, mere physical intermingling of black and white, was no antidote to segregation. They were demanding **radical** integration; but if the white community could not accept radical integration, then black men preferred to live alone and thus maintain their own dignity.

What, after all, was the ideal of integration? Contrary to what the word itself at first glance seemed to say, it was not a question of mere physical intermingling. Rather it was a question of restoring the plundered human dignity of the black man; and the chief instrument of the theft was the system of segregation. But segregation was much more than mere physical separation; and black separatists quite rightly rejected physical integration as the antidote. Much more important was that through the medium of segregation white society effectively emasculated black society by teaching it that to be white was better than to be black.

My own experience has been the common experience of the black man in America. In Selma I learned quite early that a title of respect, "Sir" or "M'am," was due to grown-up whites, but not to grown-up blacks. I remember once when my brother was bawled out by, of all people, a redneck filling-station attendant because my brother had not addressed him as "Sir." And one time at the meat market an old black lady, who knew my family and was asking how everyone was, explained to me so that the butcher could hear that I need not shake and nod my head. I could speak out my northern "yes" and "no" to her, but I would have to say "Yes, sir" and "No, sir" to Mr. McKee, the butcher. I also remember being told when I was four years old that I could not go to a certain school, which I wanted to attend, because I was not white. I remember that white people had black people to do their house work for them. I remember that I could not sit downstairs at the movie theater, or ride in front of the bus because I was not white. **No wonder I wanted to be white!** No wonder there were so many advertisements for hair straighteners and skin whiteners in black people's magazines. No wonder black dolls, aimed by toymakers at little black girls, were never a commercial success. Why shouldn't little black girls want the best—white dolls?

There precisely was the immorality of the system of segregation. It taught, and taught effectively, a whole race of people to hate themselves. It convinced the whole race of black men that they could not compete successfully in a white world. Thereby it took away our drive and our hope. White society raped our womanhood, and emasculated our manhood.

Integration then could never be the mere physical mingling of black and white men. That would be too superficial. Integration would have to be more radical; it would imply changing anything in society that robbed black men of their human dignity. In the light of this, an "integration" that **allowed** black men to live near white men would have to be unacceptable. It would be paternalistic. It would emasculate us as effectively as Jim Crowism ever did. It would presume that white is the source from which black must draw good. Such "integration" would be as immoral as segregation and for quite the same reasons.

On the other hand, a **radical** integration would mean a **mutual respect** for one another. It would make possible a cultural interchange between equals. There would be no condescension, no paternalism. The black man in these latter days has been seeking not so much to receive goods from society in a kind of eternal and degrading welfarism; rather he seeks society's acknowledgement of his own "power" to give goods to society, his "power" to be an equal partner in the building of society. Against such integration there has never been a black separatism.

27

THE GOOD SAMARITAN

"What shall I do to inherit eternal life? You shall love . . . and you will live."

The search for a fuller or for eternal life or for meaning in life is **the** basic human search. It is the same primary concern for each of us—no matter how differently each of us may go about it. After all, each of us **is different** and has a different contribution to make. There is no one way to live, no one road to heaven.

But there is one quality that all roads must share. They must be paved with love. "What must I do to inherit eternal life? You shall love . . . and you will live." Love is the root and foundation of life—God's love for us and our love for one another.

But most of us fear to love . . . . indeed, we are afraid of really living. For we know that in being selfless and generous, we can get hurt. Jesus came to show us that we need not fear getting hurt; that if we love as he loved, live as he lived, and even possibly die as he died, there will be a Resurrection. He who saves his life will lose it. I have come, he said, that you may have life, and that you may have it more abundantly. I have come that you may live, and that you may live your lives to the full. And so the sons of God should have no fear of living when a Son of God has shown the way.

We must love even our enemies, for in reality there are no enemies; we only **think** of one another as enemies (of course, that's sufficient to do the damage). What I mean is this: there is but **one** world. We depend on one another. We all need one another (perhaps in ways that we do not even realize). And therefore, we are not, naturally speaking, enemies. We have indeed the same ultimate source and the same ultimate goals. "There is but one Lord, one faith, one baptism; one God and Father of us all."

Toward one GOAL our allegiance
Toward one HOPE our faith
Toward one END (as from one SOURCE)
Toward SALVATION, Alleluia!

There is no way I can effectively say, "Stop the world, I want to get off!"
The world is ours, and we are the world's—inseparably!

And one last thought. We cannot love God at the expense of loving our
neighbor. Just because the Scripture says that we must first love God,
we cannot falsely conclude that we can love God without loving our
neighbor. No doubt, the Priest and the Levite who passed up the wounded
man in the parable of the Good Samaritan were on their way to fulfill
their duties at the Temple. They were sorry but they had to hurry on
because "God comes first." That was and is nonsense, because in passing
up the man who needed them they were passing up God. "I was wounded
and you did not help me—depart from me." Lord, when did we see you
wounded? "When you saw even the least of my brothers you saw me."

Blessed are the eyes that see what we see; for in seeing one another, we
see God. Many prophets and kings have not realized what they were
seeing; but we have been told explicitly that God the Father of all, who is
over all, and works through all, **is in us all.**

May love be the root and foundation of our lives; and may we be able to
grasp fully with all the saints the breadth and length and height and depth
of the **fullness** of God.

A REQUIEM FOR DEAD LANGUAGE

Some time ago when I was giving a retreat for the clergy of a certain archdiocese, one of the priests said in our discussion that he could not pray many of the prayers of the Mass sincerely. Most of the clergy there admitted the same. I am sympathetic to this problem. I too find it difficult to accept as my own much of the psychology and theology enshrined in the missal. Furthermore, I venture to guess that most of our contemporaries are unmoved by our liturgical language. Neither its literary style nor its theological concerns are adequate for our times.

The literary part of this problem should be solved by allowing theological **artists** to do the work so frequently left to theological **scientists**. What is more difficult to solve is the tension between traditional expressions of the faith (dogmas) and the rational demands of the modern world. Frankly, I find myself being pulled in two directions. My faith demands my loyalty. My human self demands that I be reasonable. How can I be true to my living self and the contemporary world and yet be true to the tradition that I have inherited? Can I re-interpret traditional dogmas and moral stances to suit new needs without compromising, diluting my faith?

I think I can. I remember that G. K. Chesterton said, "You don't preserve a white post by letting it alone. You repaint it each year." The true conservative must therefore be a revolutionary, willing to change external structures to preserve underlying values, willing to repaint his post to keep it white.

Is it not true that underneath the formulations of dogma (restricted by the language, knowledge and culture of the men who wrote them down) there are real transcendent values? Don't these values need to be expressed anew when the old formulations no longer speak effectively?

Is this not what St. Thomas did when he arranged the marriage of Christian thought with the thought of Plato and Aristotle? And was this not in the

spirit of Jesus? Jesus insisted that not the smallest part of a letter of the Law was to be done away with; and yet in the eyes of his contemporaries he was frequently "violating the Sabbath." He reversed the letter of the Law in favor of the woman taken in adultery. In such instances he was interpreting the Law differently from most of his contemporaries who were insisting on its preservation by a very literal interpretation.

I find absolutely no trouble in accepting the notion of moral failure, sin. I am troubled, however, by some of the treatments of sin in our liturgical and ascetical traditions. First of all, there seems to be an obsession with sin, a constant preoccupation with the need to be cleansed from sin. Frequently the implication is that we in general are terrible sinners. I simply am not convinced that I am a terrible sinner in the sense of a moral wrong-doer. I am a bit stupid, perhaps, but not a horrendous sinner. How then can I pray these incessant admissions of guilt? I simply cannot.

I am also puzzled by the notion of original sin—the general acceptance of the fact that all men are somehow vaguely **guilty,** even before they are morally responsible. This I find impossible to accept.

Then there is the sinner's relationship to God and the frequent reference to the need for propitiating God as if he were some vengeful pagan diety. If God were such, I doubt that I could warm up to him. I would find him repulsive.

I also wonder about the practice of doing penance, when that practice is one of inflicting punishment on oneself to propitiate and please God. Again, I cannot accept a sadistic God who revels in the pain of his crea- tures. My whole human self recoils from the image of a God so barbaric as to **require** the cruel death of his own Son as the price of his forgiveness.

Another problem that troubles me is this: the traditional ascetics based on the quasi-Greek supposition that spirit is perfection and that matter is imperfection; and that to be freed from matter is to be freed from all base tendencies. From this we get a monastic spirituality of withdrawing from the world in order to devote oneself to God. It implies that somehow to be concerned with creatures, even human beings, is to be divided in one's love.

We hear much talk of God's transcendence, but not enough that speaks of what we might call his general incarnation. We hear careful phrases which speak of the separate realities of heaven and earth, but what we need help with is seeing the essential unity of God's world.

Well, those are some of my problems. They were not stimulated by the reading of alien and atheistic philosophies. They were spawned by my own God-given ability to think. I am, quiet frankly, bored by the usual scientific analyses of "serious" philosophers and theologians. Any heretical doubts and any heretical solutions are purely my own. They are the result of a sincere attempt to reconcile tradition with my own peculiar requirements.

How and where I began to develop my own "cosmology" I do not know. What I do know is that it was developed over a period of many years, a bit at a time, always occasioned by some concrete traditional point that seemed unacceptable **because it stood in contradiction to some other traditional point** and my own reason. Strangely enough, generally I resolved any dilemma by resorting to some very traditional principle.

In the beginning there was God alone. Beside him there was nothing. God's was the only existence. Beside him there was only non-existence. Only God's existence is therefore ultimate proof against non-existence. Only he need exist, only he at some point existed. Only he, so to speak, kept back the onrush of the opposing non-existence.

Somehow God was moved to share his existence, **really** to share it: to allow creatures somehow to be independent of himself. He gave creatures freedom from himself—insofar as that was possible.

Now, there was risk involved in such creation. Since only God was ultimate proof against non-existence, any creature less than God was open to non-existence, to failure, to death. The failure of the creature could be twofold, moral or physical. **Success was guaranteed only by being ultimately anchored in ultimate existence, God.**

There was, however, within creatures (freed from God) the power of growing up, of maturing, of increasing their power to be, of becoming less and less a prey to non-existence, of achieving, while remaining independent, a new and closer relationship to God.

With this picture of God and his creatures in mind, I was able to resolve some of my questions. Original sin is seen not so much as guilt nor even as an inclination toward sin, but rather as the **possibility** of failure which comes with all created beings. Original sin is an unavoidable condition of all creation.

Salvation consists in being ultimately anchored in God, who alone is proof against non-existence and the forces of death. Salvation, moreover, begins when the creature first begins to be, first begins to share the life of God, when God has first pushed back the boundaries of non-being by sharing, giving generously of his own being to make another being independent of himself. The process of salvation continues as the creature grows up to its perfect state, to become itself a proof against the forces of evil, of non-existence. It grows back to God. It locks itself onto God's wavelength, the wavelength of love.

The power to give oneself freely, namely, the power to love, is **the** motive power behind the universe. There was in the beginning no force outside of God's own willingness to share. There was indeed risk in sharing; there was the risk of failure (for his creatures could indeed fail), but God's love dared, risked.

God's salvation was always open to man. However, man with his limited vision, did not see this. In fact, man was open to despair when faced by the absurdities, the incomplete salvation in this world. Man needed the possibility of ultimate salvation to be revealed to him. For Christians Jesus is this revelation from God. He is a sign of hope. Through him we come to know the saving power of God's love. Christ is our witness in his **entire** dedicated life, not merely on the cross. "God who in times past spoke to us in different ways has now spoken in the person of his son Jesus Christ."

Moreover, God reveals in Christ that he does not seek to be propitiated in any inhumane sense, but that he is a God of generosity, of forgiveness. God's mercy is always present, if we seek it with a contrite heart by returning to the "paths of righteousness," the paths of right living. Penance is not a question of deliberately inflicting pain on oneself. It is facing the trouble of living righteously. We are willing to tackle any number of difficulties to get back on the path of righteousness. We may sometimes put up with suffering—not because we like it!—but because we are willing to accept suffering for the sake of living and thereby conquering death. **Penance is not a question of mortification but of revivification.**

All of existence, even suffering, communicates something of God. Everything that exists is sacramental in a very real sense. The real presence in the Eucharist is not an isolated, magical phenomenon. Grace and nature are no longer contrary concepts. **All of nature is seen as a grace.** Union with the world, not withdrawal from it, is the way to God.

Language, including the language of religious dogmas, is a limited, imperfect tool for communication. I realize that the formulations in which I find meaning may be formulations that another person, even a contemporary, finds deficient. I am convinced, however, that all of us must have the same basic values (even though we may express them in contradictory ways) simply because we are all men. I therefore ask the Church to be tolerant in matters of dogmatic expression, to be less concerned with precise formulations, to lay aside as impractical the appellation of "heretic," to judge men no longer by the standards of arbitrary verbiage.

Rather, let us judge by the fruit of men's lives. A religious man, a believer, can no longer be considered merely a person who accepts a verbal formulation, but one **who lives righteously,** even if he calls himself an atheist. "It is not the man who says to me, 'Lord, Lord!' who shall enter the kingdom of heaven, but the man who does the will of my Father in heaven." By our fruits (not our words) we shall be known.

THE TRAGEDY OF SINCERITY

When Jesus came, he seemed to disregard certain aspects of Jewish tradition. He seemed to make light of the ceremonial laws of cleanliness. He seemed not to take the Sabbath seriously. He associated with sinners. He allowed a known prostitute to bathe his feet in perfume (and that, in public). He admitted it was all right to pay taxes to Caesar. He said that the poor were indeed blessed (when everyone knew possessions were the sign of God's blessing). When Jesus came and did all this, **he could still say that he was keeping the whole law and the prophets, and that not the smallest part of a letter of the law was to be done away with.**

How could he say that he was keeping the Law when he questioned public penance? Or when he seemed to bespeak a kind of religious indifferentism (while talking to the Samaritan woman)? Or when he seemingly attacked the very idea of a chosen people (in the parable of the marriage feast)? In such incidents, how could he say he was keeping the Law?

To us it all seems so clear. We fail to comprehend how the religious leaders of his day could have thought of him merely as a trouble-maker — a serious trouble-maker. We sometimes claim that they were insincere. But what evidence is there that they were not sincere? The tragedy is that they were sincere!

And, you know, this is the argument by which we defend the blunders of the Church: they were committed by sincere men. The men who burned

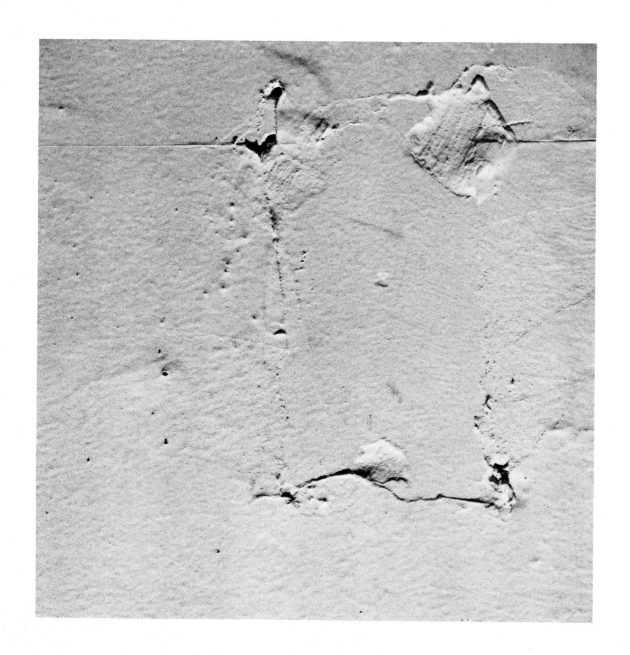

Joan of Arc were sincere, possibly more sincere than those who insisted on her sanctity in order to justify the coronation of King Charles. But this is just the point. **Sincerity is not always enough.**

We now claim that Jesus was in effect establishing a higher degree of morality, but to many of the learned men of his day, he was destroying morality.

We can draw a parallel here to what is happening in the Church and in the world today. Both inside and outside the Church theologians and philosophers are advocating a new morality which seems to many of us to be an abolition of morality. But would not most of these men claim that they want to fulfill the Law, not abolish it?

The point that I am trying to make is this: if Jesus was right in opposing the narrow legalism of his day, perhaps the prophets of "new morality" are also right. After all, the Law was made for man, not man for the Law.

What, then, is our position to be? We should, at least, be open. To be open does not mean living without standards. It describes a willingness to listen. The open person keeps in mind the limitations of language in expressing precise values. He knows that no word means **exactly** the same thing to any two people.

If we are to be open, we should not presume that another's position is really contrary to our own merely because it seems to be. We must allow, in an open dialogue, the close examination of our own standards. We must realize that our own standards are subject to change.

A knowledge of our own ignorance should help us to be humble. Humility, however, does not mean having no definite opinion. It means realizing that the world is infinitely complex. The vantage point from which each of us views the world is necessarily limited! Our vantage point is limited because we are finite and necessarily limited. (This limitation is what makes each man unique and precious.) Another's view might seem to contradict ours, only because we can't see the things that he sees from where we are standing.

There were four men of Indostan
To learning much inclined
Who went to see the elephant
Though all of them were blind
That each by observation
Might satisfy his mind

The first approached the animal
And happening to fall
Against his broad and sturdy side
At once began to bawl
"God bless us! but the elephant
Is very like a wall!"

A second feeling of the tusk
Cried, "Ha! What have we here?
This wonder of an elephant
Is very like a spear."

The poem goes on to describe how a third grasped a leg and concluded that the elephant was like a tree; and a fourth grasping the tail concluded that the elephant was like a rope. Finally the poem concludes:

And so these men of Indostan
Disputed loud and long
Though each was partly in the right
They all were in the wrong.

Each of the blind men was something of a specialist. Each grasped only a part of the truth, falsely concluding that his was the whole truth.

Each of us is something of a specialist in our knowledge of God's complex world. We need to realize that our differing views could complement one another. Our main effort then should be to see how the pieces of the puzzle fit together rather than to see how we can disprove one another.

THE PSYCHOLOGY OF SINGING

When the great ship **The Titanic** sank in the North Atlantic with terrible loss of human life, the passengers sang the old hymn, "Nearer My God to Thee." But to this day, no one has ever asked, "Why did they sing?" We have all presumed that song was the most natural thing in the world for those circumstances.

Whenever any of us gather around a campfire on a summer's evening, we invariably join in song. No one questions the reasonableness of singing, even if the songs make no sense. Moreover, I have yet to hear a so-called "non-singer" complain about having to join in.

Again, can you imagine anyone saying, "I don't mind marching in this demonstration, but why do we have to sing?" The question simply is not asked.

When we hear someone singing around the house, do we ask, "Why does he sing?" Rather, we frequently ask, "Why is he so happy?" We presume that, if one is happy, it is a natural thing to sing.

Men have sung when going to war, and have sung to celebrate peace. They have sung in sorrow as readily as in joy. They have sung both while working and while playing.

In short, the whole history of human experience reveals that singing has been almost as normal as breathing in every circumstance of life. Man has always delighted in expressing every emotion and every kind of sense, as well as non-sense, in song.

But in our time, and specifically with regard to participation in the sacred liturgy, we hear the question, "Why do I have to sing?" In the light of human experience that question is unnatural. It is as unnatural as a child's asking, "Why do I have to eat?" Yet some children do on occasion ask that question.

On such occasions some parents give the child reasons for eating. He is encouraged to eat his vegetables because they are good for him. But seldom does a lecture on proteins and vitamins move the child to eat!

On the other hand, the child does not really need the abstract, cerebral principles of nutrition. He is a natural eater. And when he does not eat, something is wrong either with the child or with the food. The wise parent will try to determine what is wrong.

So with singing. When people ask, "Why do we have to sing?" I don't think that good reasons will lead them to wholehearted liturgical singing. But we **are** singers by nature, and given the opportunity, we do sing. When we don't, something is wrong either with us or with the music.

Liturgical reform has generally been approached from entirely too cerebral a direction. Frankly, I am very skeptical of our tendency to institute liturgical reform simply by giving logical reasons for doing new things, and by issuing detailed directives. Reasons, even cogent ones, do not always convince and convert. And instructions, however detailed, cannot convey the spirit which alone will give life and dynamism to the new forms. In my opinion, only the experience of good celebration will serve to convert the unconverted. Only through experience can pastors and people grasp fully what they have been otherwise missing. Let me give you an example which does not concern the form or the liturgy itself but concerns the fact that an experience argues more effectively than do reasons and directives.

Several years ago Father Bonifaas Luykx gave me what was perhaps the first copy of the "Missa Luba" brought into this country. I gave my recording to the Sisters in our school. They played it for the children, and by the end of the week the youngsters were singing it as they had never sung church music before. When the pastor was invited to hear the children sing, he was so impressed by their enthusiasm that he decided to use the music in our church. And so, on great feasts, our children sang "Missa

Luba," because our pastor, having experienced the joy with which they sang it, wished it to be done. But can you imagine what the pastor's reaction would have been if beforehand I had come fully armed with good reasons and asked, "Father, do you think we might do this new mass—one the natives use in the Congo?" You know darn well what his reaction would have been, reasons or no reasons!

And so, I feel that those who have the job of promulgating liturgical renewal would get a far more positive response if their approach were less cerebral. If they brought to pastors and people the full, moving experience of a reformed liturgy well celebrated, the thing would argue for itself.

Once upon a time, I was certain that the solution to our music problem lay in one or two brief answers. But having questioned many people, and having thought many thoughts, I am sure that there is no simple answer to the question, "What is wrong?" Moreover, different things seem to be wrong in different places. And more than likely, a combination of things is wrong. I will try to point out the chief things that may inhibit dynamic congregational singing.

First, there is something wrong with us. As we are in some degree products of the Graeco-Roman-European-American tradition, we bring with us to our worship very limiting inhibitions. Why? In this tradition, we have not only conceptually, but, to some extent, psychologically, separated the supernatural from the natural; the spiritual from the material; the intellectual from the emotional; the spirit from the flesh; the body from the soul. The body, the flesh, the sensual, the material, the emotional, the natural are suspect—if not downright evil.

Some time ago I was visiting a well-known girls' college in the East. I was there at the invitation of the chaplain to help stimulate the program of active participation. After Mass one Sunday morning, a young lady said to the chaplain and me, "We surely enjoyed Mass this morning." My friend, the chaplain, wanted to correct her for having said she "enjoyed" Mass.

Since we have been living with this unspoken assumption that the material, the sensual and the emotional are evil, we have tried to free ourselves from the flesh. We have tried to rid ourselves of emotional involvement. We have tried to exclude these especially from worship, because on such occasions we want to be at our best—pure intellects! But we are not pure intellects, so we do not worship as whole men—or with complete involvement. When it comes to singing, we sing badly because we sing half-heartedly. A song sung half-heartedly surely prompts the question, "Why sing at all?"

When we sing only with our mouths, we are like dancers dancing only with their feet—an awkward affair. As a good dancer moves with his whole body, so must a singer sing with his whole being. A traditional Negro phrase describes this complete singing. We call it "soul-singing." Whether you say **soul singing** or **singing with guts,** you mean singing with everything that is in you. We need to lose the inhibitions that keep us from entering fully into worship. At this point in our cultural development, we should fear being too rational rather than too emotional.

Another reason we may not feel impelled to sing is that something is wrong with our ritual, or at least with our enactment of ritual. In almost every life circumstance, especially those charged with great meaning, men sing spontaneously. It is only within the artificiality of our ritual that singing is questioned.

Here is an example of what I mean when I say that our ritual does not summon a sung response as does life. When Bishop McCarthy was consecrated in Cincinnati, I was especially impressed by the very perfunctory manner in which the other bishops greeted him in the Kiss of Peace; all quite correct and according to form, but without evident meaning. But I noticed particularly Bishop Issenman, who, after going through the prescribed ritual for the Kiss or Peace, caught Bishop McCarthy by the elbow with a momentary loving, friendly grasp that had all of the meaning in it that the Kiss of Peace should have had. For some reason, he had to go beyond the rigid bounds of the prescribed ritual to express himself.

One of our chief difficulties in music is that the lack of competent music leadership frequently prevents the congregation from responding as it might. An organist with a good instrument, who plays in a leading manner, or a cantor, whole voice and personality skillfully communicate to the people, can generate a rich response. On the other hand, I know that we have all experienced the agony, the total misery, that a congregation suffers when competent music leadership is lacking. When the leader fails to accompany properly, when he does not teach the music thoroughly enough, when he antagonizes, rather than inspires, he is not likely to move the congregation to sing well.

It might be added that a good choir would be worth its weight in gold. Besides singing the beautiful music which a congregation could never sing, the choir could give backing to, and set standards for, the congregation. The choir could add harmony and variety and prevent the onslaught of monotony.

The Church generally will receive the quality of musical competence that she is willing to **afford**. Adequate salaries must be paid to musicians if they are to give the time required to improve parish musical abilities.

Besides the need for competent leadership, we also need a catholic (with a small "c") leadership, men and women who are open to all cultures. Narrow men cannot be of adequate service to a catholic community.

There is some truth in the observation that all Negroes look alike, that all Chinese music sounds the same. There is a certain sense, too, in which all standard hymns sound the same. The same form repeated time after time becomes monotonous. I would beg our creative musicians to search for new forms in which human musical needs can be satisfied. I recognize certain obstacles here. In the past, the creative Church musician has been cramped by Church restrictions. Both legal and not-so-legal restrictions were dictated by the tastes of those in authority. But now these restrictions are, thank God, disappearing.

between religious and secular music. No such thing has ever really existed. Even Gregorian chant was based on secular music. Listen to the music of the Renaissance, those motets we value so highly. I can show you bawdy love songs of the same period, in the same style. Divinely approved musical styles will prove to be just about as rare as divinely approved languages. Rather, let the musician be concerned more with the practical effect of using a particular style in a particular congregation. Not all styles will be equally useful in all congregations. Nevertheless, **no congregation can afford to forget its duty to be catholic, open to all men and their cultures.**

If the musician is not to hang on tenaciously and exclusively to traditional forms for abstract religious reasons, still less is he to do so for abstract artistic principles. Here, he is on most slippery ground. If artistic principles were any complete insurance, then artistic recipes would be possible, but the whole history of arts reads that **they are not possible.** Moreover, almost every great work of art has been produced in defiance of the principles of the preceding age. Shakespeare broke all the rules. Ben Johnson kept them all; yet whom do we honor more as a playwright today?

We want to preserve dignity and to avoid vulgarity. Of course, there is the danger, in catering to the needs of the masses, that music will be vulgar. Even worse, if we cater to the cerebral machinations of the "few," our music will be sterile. Underlying the wants of the masses is a human thirst which needs fulfillment. When this thirst is fulfilled, one can be certain he has touched reality. But underlying the wants of the closeted coterie, one often finds the momentary fashionable whim. Again I refer to the drama. No artist who has written for the chosen few has reached the artistic and humanistic heights of those who have written for the masses.

Let us gamble in the market place and risk loss for the sake of possible gain. For if the Master comes and finds us with nothing more to offer than that which we were given, he will hold us responsible. And even that which we thought we were saving will be taken away.

SING A SONG UNTO THE LORD

CLARENCE JOSEPH RIVERS

Sing a song un - to the Lord,

Al - le - lu - ia! Ev - er last - ing

is his love, ___ Al - le - lu - ia!

When the Lord restored our freedom,
We were like men dreaming.
Then our mouth was filled with laughter,
And our tongue with rejoicing.

Then they said among the nations,
"The Lord has done great things for them."
The Lord has done great things for us;
And we are glad indeed.

Let your blessings fall upon us, Lord,
Like the torrents of the Spring,
Like the rain that pours new life
Upon dry desert places.

Those that sow in tears
Shall reap in joy.
Although they go forth weeping,
Carrying the seed to be sown,
They shall come back rejoicing,
Bringing in their sheaves.

THINGS I'VE BEEN ASKED

"What do you regard as the most significant 'improvement' that has taken place in liturgical music during the past few years?"

The decree of March 7, 1967. This decree opens up the field of liturgical music to the kind of experimentation and creative efforts that heretofore were all too easily declared illegal. Of course, the decree itself is only the official manifestation of the trend in the Church to amplify and improve our notion of the "sacred." We are less and less inclined to consider any good thing as unsacred—even if it happens to be the proverbial guitar.

The result of all this is that we will be able to search more thoroughly for the kinds of music that we will need in the liturgy, no longer restrained by the rigid norms of the past which impeded the search.

"What kinds of music do we really need?"

I don't know. Nor do I think that I can give an easy formula, other than saying we must search for music that really works. And so we must try all sorts of things before we will know even a little bit about what works and what does not work.

"What do we mean by music that really works? Do you mean simple music that the congregation can sing easily? Do you mean emotional music that will stimulate a strong response?"

I mean music that expresses effectively both the intellectual and emotional content of a particular liturgical celebration. It may be relatively simple and it may be relatively complex; that doesn't matter as long as the people can sing it. Quite frequently the key to a congregation's handling pieces that are fairly difficult is that the music must be very attractive to them. For example, my "Apostles' Creed" is a difficult piece, and yet people when rightly taught find it easy simply because they like it.

In our attempts at creating music that congregations can sing easily we must avoid the danger of creating "bare" music. All too frequently even professional musicians have fallen into that trap in trying to produce music for congregations to sing, and the end result is that although they could sing the music quite easily—they don't want to sing it. The important thing is not to produce music that is "easy" or "difficult," but to produce **music that people will want to sing.**

Such music will evoke a strong or a deep response. I don't know of any mechanical way of superimposing emotion on a song. For me the emotion must arise out of the song itself. (We are not speaking here of instrumental music.) And to insure that, we must first look to the words, and their underlying idea. The idea itself must be one that is relevant, one which people can recognize as important and true, and one which they would be inclined to stamp with their approving "amen." The idea must **usually** be expressed in words and phrases which the congregation does not find awkward. At the same time, the words must have that elusive quality called poetry.

Once you have the right set of words and ideas, you must compose the melody and rhythm of the piece to fit as closely as possible the natural rhythm and inflections of the words and phrases, keeping in mind also the over-all mood of the piece.

I am trying to describe my own **ideal** working pattern here, and by no means am I presuming to set up a set of rules or a recipe for composing. In fact, I am sure that I don't follow that pattern absolutely. But when I have produced a song that **seems to have gone through those stages**, that song is most frequently one that works, and one that people will want to sing.

"So, speaking of liturgical music, you would say that superior music is that which the congregation wants to sing?"

When dealing in the arts, even the liturgical arts, I find the words "superior" and "inferior" irrelevant. It is much more to the point, most frequently, to say that this or that work was effective or ineffective. Art, contrary to the common saying, is not for its own sake, but like language itself is a means of communication. The heart of the matter is whether or not the artist is communicating effectively.

Moreover, in liturgy, we are not concerned with producing the "best in music." Rather, we want to write music that will enable people to celebrate their faith in a way that is effective for them.

However, I don't want to be quoted as saying that the artist is forever to be hemmed in by the present limitations of people. Quite to the contrary, he must help them to stretch and grow in their capabilities. By his imaginative presentation, sometimes intermingling the startling **new** with the well-worn **old,** he can lead them on to liking things they thought they would never like.

"What do you think of current popular music?"

It's great! No doubt one can find many aspects of it to criticize. But too many people throughout the world enjoy the current popular music for us to dismiss it as having little or no value. Music which touches so varied and wide a cross-section of humanity, obviously appeals to something deep within man, has a universal quality, and is the stuff out of which great art is made, when the occasional genius puts his hands to it.

Rock 'n roll has existed in the Negro popular market for the past thirty years or so, an outgrowth of certain trends in music of black American churches. But in the beginning, its influence on American popular culture was negligible precisely because white Americans did not want to associate too closely with anything identifiably Negro. In the meantime, however, the music went to Europe via recordings and via black entertainers who couldn't find employment at home. It then returned to us through the Beatles and other European pop groups. This mode of return, together with changing American attitudes, made the music acceptable. And ever since, it has been going strong. It continues also to evolve so that the superficial observer seldom sees the connection of this year's music to the pop rock of five years ago.

First there was a meeting with other elements of folk music, then came combinations with elements of jazz and even classical music. One of the results is that modern pop is bringing a much-needed tonic to the world of jazz, which has tended to develop along more esoteric lines. We now find serious students of the classical tradition, like Leonard Bernstein, studying modern pop in order to integrate it into some of their own work. Modern pop music is one of the great hopes of tomorrow's music.

"Isn't contemporary pop music more for kids than for adults?"

Kids are more likely to be open to new things than their parents, but not because kids are more stupid (as the question implies). It is simply false that adults do not find modern pop appealing. Consider the evidence: the change of music in the night clubs, the spreading of adult discotheques, the use of the music in modern musicals, the use of the music in commercials aimed at the adult market, and so forth. One radio station in Cincinnati built its format on the "older" music that adults were presumably longing for. It did not succeed. The station lost advertising and thereupon modified its policy.

"What do you regard as more important, the words or the music?"

In a given song each will have its own importance and will not be able to be played off the one against the other, as if each were members of opposing teams. In theory, the words can be considered to be more important, since it is the idea to be conveyed that will determine the form that the music will take. On the other hand, the next time you have the occasion to sing the "Happy Birthday" song, try **saying** the words throughout and see what happens. The words which in theory we considered more important turn out to be quite ineffective simply recited.

"If adults as well as young people can accept and enjoy today's music, how

do you explain the prevalence of so much liturgical music written for special groups?"

Nothing new is ever universally acceptable. Usually the young are most open to the new. The result is that a composer may simply play for a particular market where he knows that he will find easy acceptance. Moreover, the Church Fathers in the Constitution on the Liturgy acknowledged that special groups may need special consideration. The trouble is, it's always the young and "mission" countries who are presumed to need special consideration.

I did not write my music for any special age group. It appeals to a wide spectrum of people.

I do think we must avoid the present tendency to set up cultural apartheid in the church. Separate but equal facilities was an impractical arrangement for just **two** races. Think of the problem of accommodating all the cultures to be found in the average parish—grade schoolers, high schoolers, the college crowd, those over fifty, and so on. It's absurd.

I see no reason why various cultures can't exist side by side with one another in the liturgy and complement and stimulate one another. It would certainly help to avoid the monotony so prevalent in most churches. I have always made it a practice where possible to include traditional as well as contemporary musical forms in each program.

"If you were a pastor (but not Clarence Rivers) what would you do to stimulate your congregation into singing, and what would you do to insure the best in liturgical music, new and old?"

The first is a non-musical problem. I would have to make each celebration of the liturgy relevant to the lives of the people. And without getting into that, let's just say that then the music wouldn't be of paramount importance.

But, given relevant celebrations, I would hire the best musician I could find and pay him well. He would have to be well trained, talented, and open-minded. And there is another trait equally important—he would have to be able to **communicate** effectively with the congregation and the choir. Without this ability, his musical skills will be wasted. Communication is an art that our musical leadership should be trained in.

"What do you think of the practice of including secular music in the Mass?"

By secular music, I presume that you mean not merely the particular style, but a particular song like "America the Beautiful." I have no theoretical problems with this practice. If I can quote a secular poem in the homily (as often I do) why not in some appropriate place sing a secular song? I can recall preaching once on how our apparent failures are involved ultimately in the success of God. After the homily I invited the congregation to express their faith in this by joining in "We Shall Overcome." It was effective because it was fitting.

During a gathering of the Black Catholic Clergy Caucus, we put together a liturgy celebrating "soul." In commentary, song and Scripture we developed the idea that soul or vivid-life-style or full-living was at once a sign of and an effect of the dynamism of Divine Life at work in the world. In the face of so much lack of soul within the Church, we asked the question, "Can these dry bones live?" through a reading from Ezekiel. And having received an affirmative reply in that same reading, we reaffirmed our faith in the possibility of resurrection by a meditation song: "Keep in mind that Jesus Christ has died for us, and is risen from the dead. He is our saving Lord. He is joy for all ages." (Lucien Deiss, based on Timothy.) For our second reading we used several short texts from the New Testament which spoke of loving as the essence of living. Instead of the usual homily, two seminarians sang a "secular" song popularized by Nina Simone which reveled in the facts of being "young, gifted and black." It fitted perfectly because the song expressed concretely the new life, the rebirth, the soul of black America stirring once again. It worked because it was fitting.

In theory I have no problem with such practice, **but I would want to judge each instance on its own merits.** I see no sense in throwing in a secular song just to throw in a secular song. From the point of view of artistic integrity that would be just as incongruous as saying the rosary at Mass.

"What is your response to the person who argues that too much emotion deflects and subverts the proper goals of the liturgy?"

I think I would begin by asking what is meant by **too much** emotion. If he means by emotion something like "disorder," I would agree with him. But emotion does not mean disorder in itself. There is room for human emotion in every human circumstance, including the liturgy. We have been taught, however, by a tradition of puritan and Jansenistic ascetics to fear emotions; this is the main source of all questions about the place of emotion in the liturgy. Take away our heretical backgrounds and we would never have questioned the validity of celebrating the liturgy as **whole** men.

If our well-ordered service evokes an emotional response we don't have to worry. Emotion will take care of itself. It will have been aroused by the thoughts presented and it will therefore tie in with what is being celebrated. And because of it the celebration will be all the more effective.

Some time ago, I watched a friend of mine give a speech in which he took the position that "emotion does not convey thought" and therefore had no place in liturgical music which was intended to convey thought. But it was quite obvious to all present that he was being very emotional. While he was speaking, he gestured emphatically, showed great tension in his voice; his eyes were on fire—**and he held the audience spellbound.** Now, isn't that strange? He was arguing against the use of emotion to convey thought, but was being all the more effective and persuasive **precisely because he was using emotion.** There's the danger in emotion! It can be used for the wrong purposes, like arguing against itself. But we do not avoid using good things simply because there is some remote danger involved in their use.

"Once we have licked the music problem, do you think that our liturgical

problems will have been mostly solved?"

By no means. In fact, as I said before, if our liturgy really meant something to people, we wouldn't be so preoccupied with questions like what music to use. Music may help to make the liturgy come alive; even more so will a "live" liturgy make some quite tepid music come alive. For example: no one, not even the musicians who were involved, worried about the quality of music used during the heyday of the civil rights demonstrations. When the quality of the singing was poor, the music still seemed to thunder with all the power of an hallelujah chorus. "The Barrel Organ," a poem by Alfred Noyes, is quite to the point when it says, ". . . though the music's not immortal, the world has made it sweet and fulfills it with the harmonies that make a song complete . . ."

When our liturgies are so effectively constructed, so effectively performed, and so oriented toward our lives that they are real celebrations of things that mean something to us, some of our preoccupations, like what kind of music to use, will begin to seem absurd.

"Are you saying that liturgical renewal ought to be concerned with more essential things than with music?"

Music is definitely a justifiable concern, but there are other concerns which we have not yet begun to touch; for example, the theology and the psychology of the prayers of the Mass. We still talk of "propitiating" God as if he were some sadistic god whose anger is assuaged only by masochistic bloodletting by his people. If God were like that, very frankly, I wouldn't bother with him. So how can I say prayers that talk of "propitiation?" I don't, or else I associate different thoughts with those words.

Consider another example: the relationship between the Church and the world, between liturgy and life. Liturgical language still seems to set these at poles rather than at peace, so that it is difficult, unless one strains, to see any connection between ideas associated with "liturgy" and ideas associated with "life." Our communion service, for instance, is not enunciated so that it makes clear that the man who seeks union with God must live in holy communion with his neighbor.

Liturgical law itself needs to be re-oriented. The law still takes for granted that necessary liturgical experiments can be legislated in detail, and that no individual priest should change the slightest detail without explicit legal approbation. This rigidity leads directly to many liturgical absurdities. The solution lies not in rigid norms but in helping our liturgical leaders to develop the necessary artistic and theological "taste" so that they can effectively apply official norms to particular circumstances.

Liturgical reform has a long way to go.

THE REVOLUTIONARY CHRIST

Biblical religion is worldly. (This is not to say the Scriptures do not show a healthy appreciation of the uniqueness of God or that the Bible minimizes the transcendence of God.) The preoccupation of the Gospel with "the kingdom of heaven" or "the kingdom of God" is not a concern with the "afterlife." The kingdom of heaven in the New Testament is "the rule of God in **this** life." The kingdom of heaven is **this world acting according to the divine plan,** or in other words, "things as they ought to be."

As long as anything remains undone, the kingdom of heaven is unfinished, still to be built. The kingdom will never be perfectly synonymous with "the world" until the world becomes perfect. "Heirs of the kingdom of God" are therefore constantly building and rebuilding, forming and reforming their civilization. Their eye is on the future. They are called to be prophets, called to speak in behalf of God's kingdom. As such, as speakers and doers in behalf of an unfinished kingdom and a new social order, prophets are in the best sense of the word "revolutionaries."

The biblical tradition is committed to the past only insofar as it moves

toward a better future. Those who believe in the biblical tradition should never be satisfied with the status quo. Our world is always in need of formation and reformation. The Roman Catholic Church herself, in the Vatican Council, made her own the cry of the Protestant Revolution: "Ecclesia semper reformanda est." The Church must be continually re-formed.

Our call as Christians is similar to the call of our nation as it was conceived by certain of her founding fathers. I have seen in our Capitol a reproduction of an eighteenth-century fireplace. On it the rods and the axe, symbols of governmental authority and stability, **were surmounted by the nightcap,** the symbol in those days of revolution. **Reform was to be the style of our government itself.** Government was not to be the protector of the status quo.

So whether we think of ourselves as Americans or as heirs of the Bible, we are the heirs of a revolutionary tradition, and to be true to either we must be willing to leave the good to seek the better. But let us be honest with ourselves; we are not true to our traditions. Most of the stands that most of us take on most issues would in other times have identified us with the enemy. We would have considered most of our founding fathers extremists. We may have agreed with Pilate and certain of the religious leaders of Jerusalem that Jesus was a troublemaker and that he was stirring people up too much.

Jesus was a troublemaker. The word describes him accurately. He came into a society which believed that wealth was a sign of God's blessing and that poverty was an affliction for sin. Yet he said, "Blessed are the poor." He came into a prudish society which said that no gentleman, no nice man, would associate with a prostitute (in public), and **he allowed a known prostitute to pay him personal service in the sight of everyone.** He came into a society which believed in just wars and holy wars of liberation, a society that under violent oppression longed for an opposing violence to set things right, who thought of the Messiah as a sword-swinging warrior, and he said, "Blessed are the peacemakers." He came into a religious society and **broke the Sabbath,** and **criticized religious leaders in public,** and **ridiculed certain penitential customs,** preached what some people might call religious indifferentism, saying that he looked forward to the day when men no longer prayed in temples of any denomination but would worship the Father in spirit and in truth. He came into a society that valued the luxury of hate and said that we could not afford to hate. Love your enemy, he said, do good to him who hurts you.

He came into a world very much like our own, and took stands that most of us would have considered idealistic or impractical or unrealistic. He says in the parable of the vineyard that the world is to be run on generosity, not legal justice. Now how many of us are ready to buy that bit? We think that the fumbling attempts of the early Church to be communistic and pacifistic were quite naive. Would we have considered Jesus dangerous? Would we have been quite pleased when he was finally picked up on a capital charge? Would we have cried "Free Barrabas! Crucify Jesus!"?

Like the children of Israel called out of bondage to a new freedom in a promised land, we can find the Christian pilgrimage difficult. We too can yearn again for the flesh pots of Egypt, preferring enslavement when the price of freedom is hunger for a time. In spite of our having gone through the rituals of liberation, of having passed through the sea of baptism and having eaten the food of God, we are not yet free heirs and builders of the kingdom, pleasing to God. We must become like Jesus, dedicated humane reformers of our own selves and of our society.

LITURGICAL FETISHES

Fetish: an object believed to have magical power to protect or aid its owner; an object regarded with extravagant trust; an object of irrational or obsessive devotion.

We regard ourselves as more "sophisticated" than the primitive people of ages past or in certain other parts of our world today. We do not see ourselves as superstitious or as believers in magic. We tell ourselves that rabbits' feet, four-leaf clovers and horseshoes are merely quaint relics, fond reminders of a past when people really believed in that sort of thing. Yet we do regard some things with excessive trust and devotion. Example: clerical dress. Those who naively fear its curse, wanting naively to abolish it altogether, are just as superstitious as those who trust its goodness, wanting to retain it entirely. Our Lord asks us to notice the flowers in the field when we become too worried and fussy about what to wear. I believe Jesus would laugh at our fetishes as we search for adequate liturgical expression. This chapter is about some of those fetishes.

OF SOUND AND SILENCE

During the era of passive participation there was a "silent prayer" fetish. Somehow, lack-of-sound became the equivalent of deep devotion and reverence. Now in the era of active participation, we sometimes make the number of decibles produced the sole measure of our "joy in the Lord." Neither position, of course, is absolutely right nor absolutely wrong. The moment of silent prayer is often enhanced if the meditation period is preceded by a rousing song. Instrumental music in the background can be a powerful aid to the imagination. On the other hand, experience tells us that to be always hearing noises (even intelligible ones) is soon to be hearing nothing.

If our fetish is for passive participation, we need to remember that the human being is not a sponge, not merely a receiver. He is above all, a doer.

On the other hand, active participation can lead to the fetish of having **everybody** do **everything** all the time. Some things are more adequately done for the whole celebrating community by solo performance. For example, it is highly unlikely that the whole congregation, reading the Gospel aloud together, will be as effective as a solo reader. The dialogue homily (which some cynic has called "pooled ignorance") can be quite effective. Under certain circumstances, however, it makes no sense: when the crowd is too large and unwieldy or when acoustics prevent the assembled people from speaking to and hearing one another clearly. Also, often the particular occasion demands something more artistically integrated than the usual dialogue is.

GATHERING AROUND THE ALTAR

As deacons in the seminary, we were advised by a seminary official to maintain a certain reserve, a certain aloofness from the other students—in order to solicit the proper respect for our status. In much the same way the Church had for sometime sought to solicit the proper respect for the sanctuary by keeping people away from it. The veil of the temple, split on the first Good Friday, was only a source of rhetoric—empty of practical results.

When he was finally invited to come closer, quite naturally the average churchgoer was thrilled—the experience was not unlike tasting a delicious forbidden fruit. "Let's gather around the altar," said some retreat master and forty or fifty people were able to "view" the Mass from a perspective that was new and moving. It was a valid, effective, reasonable thing to do. There are, however, times when we should not gather around the altar. I remember that one time, at the offertory, the chaplain of a particular college invited some two hundred of us to gather around the altar **as closely as possible.** When some hesitated two feet or so from the table, he insisted that they come right up to the edge of the table. It made little sense. The first ten or fifteen people effectively blocked anybody else from seeing the altar. Simply being close to the altar had become a fetish. The chaplain, following a rule to increase "visibility," made visible communication between celebrant and congregation impossible. Something similar happens when an altar is taken from a raised platform where it was visible to the whole congregation and is "brought closer" by placing it on the floor level where it is visible only to the very first rows. The altar in effect was "closer" when it was farther away.

"PROPER" LANGUAGE

All language (even analytical language) is a matter of metaphor, a matter of poetry. The fundamentalist mind, which reads all language literally, almost always stands in danger of confusing "the sign" with "the thing signified." The fundamentalist will find it difficult to see that **the very same reality can be represented by different signs.** The fundamentalist makes the mistake of thinking that preserving a particular sign is equivalent to preserving the real thing. However, even visible creation, the sign of our Creator is always changing. As we are reminded by Tennyson in the **Idylls of the King:** "The old order changeth, giving place to new; and God fulfills himself in many ways."

Rubrical Words

Whether we are concerned with Aristotle's **Poetics** or with rubrical prescriptions of the Roman rite, we are dealing with an attempt to regulate artistic results by setting standards. In either case, we make a fetish of the rules if we insist on following them slavishly, as if their mere enactment would automatically guarantee results. Such is not the case. Witness, for example, the relative failure of neoclassic literature which made a point of following all the rules. The failure of all such rule-worship is in its "fundamentalism." When one speaks of balance, it is sheer fundamentalism to think only of a design with two equalized sides, such as the human face. "Balance" obviously means something deeper than that. Balance is also achieved by imbalance, as when a woman sets a vase of flowers at one end of a shelf rather than at the center or when an artist places a circle in one corner of a page instead of in the center.

We should, then, consider the **purpose** of liturgical rubrics or directives instead of concentrating on their mere literal statement.

There are, I think three basic reasons for liturgical rubrics: to preserve tradition, to insure standards of performance, to promote universality. Now a slavish following of the rules—expecting them to work magic—will often produce the very opposite results.

Tradition is not preserved by simply not changing. For example, Latin was introduced into Western liturgy to make the liturgy intelligible to people who no longer spoke Greek. To preserve Latin liturgy in the name of tradition when people no longer spoke Latin was really untraditional—if we consider the **purpose** for which the Latin liturgy was initiated.

High standards of artistic performance cannot be rigidly legislated. Think of the poor showing created when priests followed exactly the prescriptions for extending their hands during prayer. Instead of preserving an acceptable standard, this rigid rule-following created ridiculous gestures.

Finally, universality should not be confused with uniformity. Mechanically uniform ceremonials do not necessarily deliver a uniform message. For instance, white is traditionally used for feasts of great joy in the Roman rite; but in parts of the Orient, white is the color for mourning.

Obviously, liturgical rubrics work no magic and insure no results. We need to be more imaginative.

Doctrinal Words

Dogmas attempt to express in words our "traditional" convictions, our faith about the nature of the world, about the ultimate values of life. But we must not hold them too dear. St. Thomas Aquinas spent his life trying to express his faith in adequate words, and is reputed to have called his acknowledged monumental work "a thing of straw." All our attempts at analyzing and codifying reality but scratch the surface. Thomas Aquinas was wise enough to realize that. Not so wise were the people who burnt his books in the streets of Paris as heresy, and the people who later canonized his thoughts as the only valid formulation of the faith. Language is metaphorical. **Different signs can represent the very same reality.** Unless we keep this in mind, we may make heresy hunting a fetish. We can have an obsessive devotion to a particular set of doctrinal signs, refusing to admit the validity of other signs. Within our own dogmatic traditions we already have two sets of signs that would be contradictory if we insisted on conceiving of either as absolute and unchanging statements of the truth. I refer to the Jewish concepts of our biblical tradition, in contrast to the Greek concepts of our scholastic tradition.

The thirteenth-century biblicists found it hard to accept scholastic notions as valid expressions of Christian faith; so they burned the books of Thomas Aquinas. Latter day scholastics find it hard to accept modern concepts; so they fear heresy, even when contemporary theologians return to expressing the faith in biblical terms. When will we learn that the words of our dogmas have their limitations? To fix on any statement as the last word about reality is to create one more fetish.

SMALL GROUP CELEBRATIONS

One frequently hears nowadays that the large size of parish liturgies militates against good celebrations. Only smaller, more intimate groups make for better liturgies. This position makes a fetish out of size. Nothing magic happens when we merely reduce (or for that matter when we merely build up) the size of the congregation. If the liturgy of a large gathering fails to "come off," the failure is not in the size of the group. The problem is in the manner of the performance. Somehow, the manner did not suit the size. On the other hand, the liturgy in small gatherings will not work either unless the manner of the celebration is appropriate. My own experience is that liturgies in gatherings of three thousand to five thousand, like the liturgies I have been privileged to share with members of the Christian Family Movement at Notre Dame, are just as effective as some of the moving celebra-

tions that have been shared by a few friends in my home.

On the other hand, I have participated in home liturgies that were as disastrously dull as anything that ever happened in a parish church. Where does one get the "magic" of music in a small group that is musically untalented? How does one find the special "power" in small groups that is generated only by large masses of people singing and reciting in unison? The small group shares a different kind of power. Intimacy can have a "magic" of its own that can replace the charms of music. Under some circumstances a quietly spoken word is as powerful as the roaring acclamation of a crowd.

Both large and small celebrations can be effective. Neither is exclusively so. We need both.

OF INSTRUMENTAL MONOMANIA

When the organ was introduced into Christian worship, it was called by some Church Father (who undoubtedly preferred lyres and drums and flutes) "the instrument of the Devil." Later the organ came to be "the queen of all instruments" and the **only** sacred one. For heaven's sake, let's not make the same mistake with the guitar (especially the poorly played guitar). There is a growing irrational reverence for the guitar. If the situation gets any worse, I expect to hear the guitar eulogized one day soon as "an essentially humble instrument—fitting for the pilgrim Church." As a metaphor, that's not a completely hopeless idea; but as an absolute, of course, it is nonsense! Use the piano, use brass horns, reeds, strings and drums, use even the organ. Avoid instrumental monomania! The only magic to be sought is the magic of excellent performance—regardless of the instrument.

THE EUCHARIST

The Mass itself, the memorial of Christ's generous living is no doubt the central Christian celebration. But even the Mass can become a fetish.

Is it wise to make daily or even weekly Mass a universal ideal? Does such frequent repetition **prevent** it from being special? Should we have a Mass as "the ideal setting" for weddings, funerals and baptisms?

As central as the Mass is, we should not ask it to do everything on every occasion.

We can make a fetish or a gimmick of the folk as well as the classical, of the modern as well as of the ancient. Any good thing can be clung to irrationally. However, we must not stop seeking and using good things in fear of fetish. So please don't make a fetish out of anything I've said!

THE FETISH OF WANTING A KING

Since the institution of the Feast of Christ the King, in hundreds of thousands of Churches throughout the world, millions of Catholics have given honor to a Christ depicted in royal robes, crowned in Gold, with the world bowing in humble submission before him. And few of us have bothered to wonder whether or not this celebration might be in some respects improper. I would like to suggest that this celebration, **as we have known it,** is improper.

First of all, kings have for the most part been unacceptable. Even in the Old Testament when the people came to Samuel and demanded that they be given a king just like the other nations, God warned them that kings would be unacceptable and that they should trust in his rule. But the people insisted and so they got one.

But by this time in history we have stopped wanting kings to rule us. We have chased them into exile. We have executed a few. And the few that are left are only ceremonial, having little real power. The image of kings is, on the whole, a very bad image. So why do we insist on putting the image onto Christ, and then expect the world to accept the Christ that we offer?

Have we not frequently preached that a thing is right simply because Christ **wills** it? To preach that is to expect submission to tyranny. To preach that is to depict Christ as a tyrant. To project that image of Christ is to make him unacceptable to men who value their freedom.

The Bible does refer to Christ as King. Christ himself admitted to kingship in the Gospel, but he insisted that his kingdom was **not of this world, that is, not as you are accustomed to think.** Although the title is used, it carries with it none of the usual trappings of kingship. He refused to take on the role of Messiah (as they thought of a messiah): ". . . and when he perceived that they would make him king, he fled himself alone, into the mountains." In the Garden of Gethsemane, he again refused a "worldly" kingdom, demanding that Peter put up his sword: "If my kingdom were of this world, my Father would have sent an army."

Here was a king who cared nothing about socially acceptable dignity, but who associated with social outcasts and sinners. Here was a king who did care for people. Moved by their hunger, he multiplied loaves in their behalf. Here was a king who cared for people who were in sorrow; he raised loved ones from the dead. Here was a king who cared for people who were in pain; he drove out devils and cured diseases. Here was a king whose works, whose miracles, **were not to be taken as a sign of power, but as a token of love.** Here was a king who washed the feet of his disciples and who said, "If I have done so to you, so should you be willing to wash the feet of one another." Here was a king who came not to be served, but to serve.

If there has been anything good in our celebration of the Feast of Christ the King, it has been our loyalty to him and our care for his world-wide "kingdom." But remember, our loyalty must be a question of deeds, of service to one another even as he taught us. Strangely enough, we spread his influence across the world, not in the manner of kings who spread their influence by aggressive power—but by serving the needs of our fellow men.

FACING THE FUTURE

In the Peace Corps and Vista, significant numbers of people are dedicating their lives to the betterment of world-wide neighborhoods. In the United Nations, men are striving, however imperfectly, to build a world community. Statesmen are beginning to promote the distribution of wealth to all people. All of these developments lead me to believe that the moral state of the world is better than ever.

On the other hand, we have not become as morally perfect as we need to be to satisfy the demands of the times. The present and the future call us to an even greater moral perfection.

Already we are being called upon to reconsider the basic motivational force of our government, of our social contract. We have been operating on the premise that legal justice is an adequate concept for social government. However, "to each man what he earns" begins now to be less and less equal to "what each man deserves." We are learning that society cannot be healthy unless all men in that society attain a certain standard of living, whether they have in the narrow sense earned it or not. In international affairs we are learning that an enemy becomes someone with whom we reason and negotiate, because our mutual possession of "ultimate weapons" forces us to abandon heaping on our enemy his "just deserts." In other words, we are learning to replace the concept of legal justice with something that approaches love as the motivational force in society. For the present, at least, we have not fully accepted this, nor have we realized where we are being forced to go. We are being constrained by circumstances, to act as if we loved, not realizing that it is love that we are called upon to practice.

Already the world is so densely populated and so closely knit by communication and transportation that it is impossible to isolate oneself completely from any other individual, tribe or nation. The crowded tenements of New York are linked with the rural Middle West and the mountainous West Coast by a few minutes of jet travel. And the starving millions of India and

China will soon be as close as the beggars on the streets of Chicago. The words of John Donne ring truer than ever before: "No man is an island entire of itself; and any man's death diminishes me, because I am involved in mankind."

We are living in a world so complex that centralized government control is becoming more and more useless. In these circumstances organized society sorely needs individuals with a highly developed sense of responsibility. In one way we are entering an age of unparalleled freedom; in another sense, we are entering a time when free men must become slaves of duty. We are not prepared for social life in these times unless we resolve the conflict between the controls of legitimate authority and the necessary freedom of individuals.

We are living in an age in which pat answers learned in school are useless. Our knowledge of the world is growing fast. Our technology is growing even faster. Now the man of one skill will be disappearing like the dinosaur, unable to cope with the new world. Education must take a new twist. It must prepare men to enter unknown situations with imagination and intelligence and to fashion new worlds from day to day.

An age of such rapid change can belong only to those who have a sense of adventure, who are willing to take risks for greater gains, who are willing to accept the new alongside the old—or even in the place of the old. In other words, the middle-class, security-conscious mentality will be completely out of place. Already young people are looking for jobs with "significance," not merely jobs where they can accumulate moderate wealth.

My greatest fear in all this is that our capacity for technological growth has far outstripped our capacity for moral and psychological growth.

My other worry, as a Christian, is that we of the Churches are not on the cutting edge of modern movements. Biblical religions have something to say to modern man. The Bible has already described the ideals toward which society is blindly striving.

Unfortunately, we of the Church are not being good witnesses. We are still too preoccupied with saving our own selves. We need to realize that saving the world is at least a part of the job of saving self. We are too smug, too self-righteous, too much enthralled by the fact that we are a chosen people, and not attentive enough to the fact that all chosen people are dispensable: "Out of these very stones, I can raise up children to Abraham." Let us admit with humility that the agnostic and the atheist have frequently been much more responsive to the Spirit in building a new world. One reason the Church seems unresponsive lies in the fact that she has become an "establishment," with the consequent tendency to stifle the sometimes strident voice of prophecy.

Throughout the history of salvation, as recorded in scripture, prophecy is central to moral growth. The prophets were the social conscience throughout Old Testament history. In the New Testament Jesus is known as a prophet and teacher. The teaching ministry was the prime concern of the Apostles. Only after the Church became a part of the establishment, through Constantine and Charlemagne, did the priest's role become more highly valued than the prophet's role.

The unfortunate result was that the Church, which started out with high revolutionary ideals (in the best sense of these words) and which should have continued to be a prime mover in social reform, was all too often the guardian of an unchristian status quo—standing in the way of reform, or at best, becoming a reluctant follower instead of a leader. This was inevitable because the voice of prophecy was neglected and even suppressed. Virtues were preached to promote establishment interests, virtues such as obedience to those in authority, and "pious" intolerance of all dissent. And so, the servant Church—which should have been willing, like Christ, to wash feet—became triumphalist. Unlike Christ this Church was willing to be crowned King. (Even the papacy and the episcopacy began to be conceived in terms of **monarchical** authority.)

If the Church is to continue reform within itself and make itself a witness to ideals needed in the world, the voice of prophecy must be heard once more.

In a world frequently swamped in needless suffering, where men are crying out in Job-like anguish for some answer, **God is silent except when he speaks through our lives.** Somehow, we of the Church must live so as to reveal that there is an ultimate meaning to the world.

In a world where death is commonplace, the prophet must suggest by the way he lives that life is to be faced and lived fully even at the risk of death. The prophet must also suggest that life transcends the narrow apparent boundaries of "this world" and ultimately overcomes death.

In our world a smile is so often considered the sign of an empty mind. A long face or a frown is often thought to betoken deep thought. Even in the Church, tears are considered more proper than laughter. In such a world, the prophet of God's salvation must suggest that joy is the possession of those who believe in the love of God, who indeed believe in God's world.

Strangely enough, the prophet among us must continually remind us that the Church is not merely a kind of spiritual filling-station where one drives in to get high octane graces. The Church is the continuation in time of the Incarnation, the continuing presence of Christ on earth. We must remember why Jesus came to earth: not, as we have sometimes imagined, to satisfy the vengeance of some dreadful God. Christ came that man might come to know in human terms how much God loved the world and how far God was willing to go to save the world.

The prophet within the priest must continually remind the priest that we do not bear witness merely by faithful attendance at Mass and by receiving the sacraments. Religion not accompanied by a decent social life has been tried before and has been repeatedly condemned by the prophets of the Old and the New Testaments.

All social groups, human institutions, civil and religious establishments need prophets because the very good points of any orderly society can be its own undoing. Any society will become inhumane whose reverence for abstract dogmatic principles outweighs its concern for real people in concrete (sometimes compromising) situations. Any society (of the right or of the left) will become totalitarian if its order is based ultimately on laws (however good!) rather than on **a moral people.** Any society which makes order equivalent to sameness-in-its-citizens, that refuses to tolerate the eccentricities of prophets, will finally reduce its citizens to automatons.

The voice of prophecy throughout Biblical tradition has stimulated a sometimes sluggish people to cast off the slavery of the past; to seek as pilgrims a new and better land; to serve God by **serving one another;** to build and rebuild cities with the unshakeable stones of righteous social living; to look upon **different** brothers as different **members** of the whole body, needing one another, suffering and rejoicing with one another.

A society that has no prophets has no future.

LIVING, DYING AND RISING: A MATTER OF LOVING

"We have passed out of death and into life—because we love our brothers . . . not just in words or mere talk but in deed and in truth." (1 John 3, 14-18)

At the very dawn of his intelligence man came to know death. At first he saw it as the ending of life, an end that was inescapable yet greatly undesirable. Precisely because it was undesirable, man faced death with the hope that what he saw of death was only an appearance, that death might not be the end, that somehow life might continue beyond the grave. And so men fashioned a great many theories about the possibility of life beyond death to bolster their growing hope. Then, for us, through Jesus Christ, the hope became a promise.

Out of that promise, St. Paul assured us that if we were united to Christ in the likeness of his death, we would continue to be united to Christ in the likeness of his resurrection. "If we believe," Paul wrote to the Thessalonians, "that Jesus died and yet rose, so also God will bring forth with him all who have fallen asleep believing in Jesus." With such assurance our attitude toward death is slowly evolving into a more positive disposition.

Now I would like to suggest that we extend our vision of life, of anti-death, of resurrection even further. I would like to suggest that the promise of resurrection was not merely concerned with the afterlife. Our resurrection, our delivery from the grave, begins even in this life.

I see death itself as preceding and accompanying life. Our deliverance from non-existence by the gift of life is the first step in our deliverance from death. But even after that first step, anything that stands in the way of a **full** life partakes of death, is a kind of death. Anything that prevents men from living as full, free, grown-up sons of God partakes of death, is a kind of death. Anything that stands in the way of the world's further development is a kind of death.

Sin—moral failure—is death. To struggle against moral failure is to fight one's way out of a grave. Deliverance from sin is a resurrection. Lack of food, shelter and recreation is death, and deliverance from poverty is a resurrection. The darkness of ignorance is its own special death, and the sunrise of knowledge is an Easter dawning. Lack of freedom is death and every defeat of oppression, slavery and tyranny is a resurrection victory.

Every effort that contributes to human progress is a further manifestation of unquenchable divine life, filling the world. When a new poem is written, when a new song is sung, when a disease is cured, when a new machine is perfected, life is increased in the world and resurrection is closer to realization even in this life.

You and I cannot touch directly the life beyond the grave. We have the power within our hands, however, to lift the veil of death that covers this world. If we love in deed and in truth, if our love is real and active. We can feed the hungry, shelter the homeless, care for the fatherless. We can visit the sick, and cure the diseased. We can bring compassion to those in distress and lift burdens from the backs of the oppressed. We can teach the ignorant. The power of the life of God is within us. We can perform the resurrection miracle in unspectacular ways for one another day after day, if our love is real and active, if we love in deed and in truth.

In the beginning, time before time was, there was God—the Life Force, Eternal Resurrection. Outside of his existence there was no existence. Outside of his life there was only death. He was alone. But to be alone, inverted, was not in him because he **cared,** he **loved.** And caring he begot, begetting all that now has come to be, pushing back the boundaries of death and non-existence by sharing in deed and in truth. And therefore, we can say that **God is love,** for he was that Life that cared so much that he could not live alone but was bound to share his living. He was forced by love to share his life. His love made him a life force.

It is love, therefore, which makes the world go. Let us join the cause of God against death. By force of love, by virtue of caring, let us share our lives, give of our existence that the boundaries of death are pushed back even further. Let us help others to pass from death to fuller life even in this world. Then we too shall pass from death to eternal life.

I was hungry and you fed me, naked and you clothed me, ignorant and you taught me, wounded and you healed me, lonesome and you came to me, homeless and you let me come to you, in despair and you gave me hope. Come and possess the kingdom; enter eternal union with eternal life!

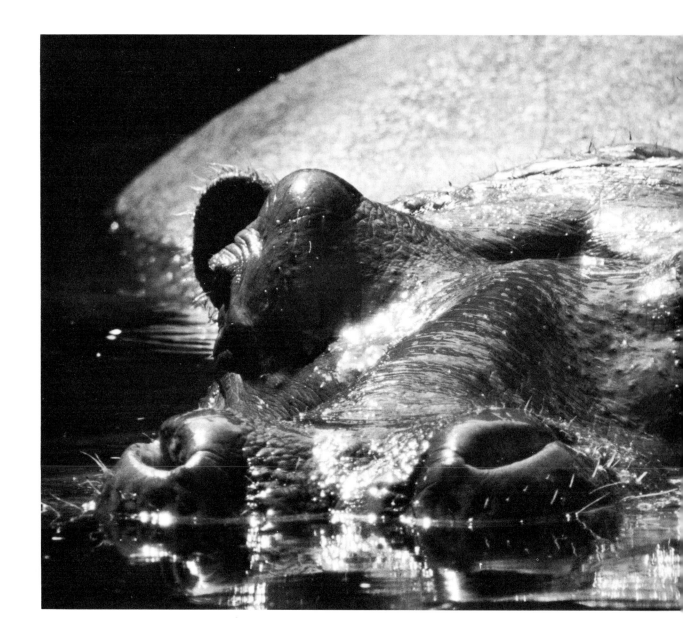

PHOTO CREDITS

EPILOGUE

"Blessed are the meek, for they shall inherit the earth."

In the unrecorded beginnings, mankind learned to use power and force and violence to solve his problems. With violence he killed his food, and with violence he defended his kill, and the aggressive survived, and the strongest and most aggressive became leaders; warriors became kings.

In our warrior cultures might and right became synonymous. Righteousness and justice were established in trials by combat. God, it was presumed, was on the side of the victor.

We are still living in the warrior age. Might and power and violence are still **the** way to establish right. School boys still consider it manly to defend one's honor by resorting to fists; and they do not learn this from their peers —their elders have called boxing the manly art. Indeed, how many times have you heard it said that our honor is at stake in Vietnam (not merely the honor of living up to one's pledged word, but the warrior's honor of never walking away from a fight)?

Paradoxically, right alongside our cult of violence, a contrary ideal sprang up and still survives. In biblical tradition the barren woman is given the hope of vindication in the face of her prolific rival. Slaves are freed and masters are enslaved. The hungry are filled and the sated left hungry. The mighty are put down from their thrones, and the lowly are raised up. The powerful are put down and the powerless are exalted. The meek, not the aggressive, inherit the earth.

There is born the paradox of the Cross! Those condemned to death may possess eternal life.

"The language of the cross may be illogical to those who are not on the way to salvation; but those of us who are on the way see it as God's power to save. As Scripture says: "I shall destroy the wisdom of the wise and bring to nothing all the learning of the learned. Where are the philosophers now? Where are the scribes? Where are any of our thinkers today? Do you see now how God has shown up the foolishness of human wisdom? If it was God's wisdom that human wisdom should not know God, it was because God wanted to save those who have faith through the foolishness of the message that we preach. And so, while the Jews demand miracles and the Greeks look for wisdom, here we are preaching a crucified Christ; to the Jews a stumbling block, to the Greeks madness; but to those who have been called, whether they are Jews or Greeks, a Christ who is the power and the wisdom of God. For God's foolishness is wiser than human wisdom, and God's weakness is stronger than human strength.

Take yourselves for instance, brothers, at the time when you were called: how many of you were wise in the ordinary sense of the word, how many were of influential people, or came from noble families? No—it was **to shame the wise** that **God chose what is foolish** by human reckoning, and **to shame what is strong** that he **chose what is weak** by human reckoning; those whom the world thinks common and contemptible are the ones that God has chosen —those who are nothing at all to show up those who are everything." (1 Corinthians 1, 18-29)

Even in **Look** magazine, there was recently the prophecy that during the Seventies "power" would go out of style in American politics. "Blessed are the meek; they shall inherit the earth."

Martin Luther King believed in that prophetic dream, and saw the possibility of a righteous society, one based on mutual caring. "The Holy Ghost," he said, "is the community-creating reality that moves through history." In other words: God's love, operative through us, will create community, will build up society. We cannot ultimately depend on the law and order of warrior cultures.

Now, to tell warriors to put away their swords when they have with their swords established a kind of order—the only order experienced so far—is to threaten the very existence of order (in their eyes). To tell men convinced, like the Senator in Drew Pearson's novel, that selfish interest, "controlled greed," is the building material of the social structure—to tell such a man that generosity must be the motive force of social cooperation—will at least invite his laughter. But if he thinks you're serious, and that you may be persuasive, he will then brand you as a troublemaker, especially if you put your powers of persuasion on the side of the oppressed. And even though such a troublemaker tells his followers to put up their swords, that troublemaker runs the risk of death. Bernard Shaw said that Christ would have to be crucified again in every generation to save those who have no imagination. And so Martin Luther King is dead.

And though we may admire Dr. King and the prophetic tradition out of which he spoke, **we are nonetheless still warriors.**

I, for one, am not willing to give up the use of violence until everyone else has given it up. I cannot dispossess myself of the notion that, under certain desperate circumstances where the forces against me will not yield to reason, violence is the way out. A few weeks ago I was attacked by a dog, a huge Weimaraner. After he had sunk his fangs into my arm and my back—and was ready to spring again—I did not turn around to reason with him. I kicked him in the mouth, which held him off until his owner came and pulled him away.

I feel that human beings are potentially reasonable, but are frequently as unreasoning as mad dogs. And under certain desperate circumstances I reserve the right to defend my life, if necessary, with violent means. And I think that most of you would feel likewise.

And I would like to say to Mahatma Gandhi: yes,your techniques worked with the British, but how would they have worked against a Hitler already entrenched in power? I have every reason to believe that a man like Stalin might order his tanks to move right over the outstretched supplicating bodies of Hungarians or Czechoslovakians, if he thought the interest of the Kremlin demanded it—world opinion be damned. Didn't George Wallace threaten to run his car over the prostrate bodies of protesters? Again, I think that most of you would ask similar questions.

I have some reservations about embarking on unilateral disarmament; or about the abolition of our armed forces, or even armed policemen. And I think that most of you have the same reservations. Without the National Guard the high school in Little Rock would still be totally segregated; and George Wallace would still be standing in the doorway of the University of Alabama.

You and I might ask Dr. King how far non-violence would have taken him if Bull Connor and Jim Clark had not been threatened with national police forces more powerful than their own local ones. And again you and I might agree.

But now, having asked similar questions, having made the same reservations, having been motivated by the same limited experience to have the same fears, we must admit that we are in a cul-de-sac, a dead end. Because, agree as we will on certain generalities, we are all different. We are bound to have many disagreements. And when those disagreements are hot and ultimate, in a world where isolation has become impossible and interdependence is a physical necessity, we may kill one another—or at the very least enslave and oppress one another.

When our tools were only sticks and stones, the damage that we warriors might have inflicted on one another was limited. But now we can arm ourselves with nuclear fission and genetic engineering and mind controlling techniques. Even with our present, primitive medicine-man psychology we can brainwash. We cannot maintain twentieth-century technology alongside cave man, warrior morality, for if we do, we will destroy ourselves. We were warned by John F. Kennedy: "Unless man can match his strides in weaponry and technology with equal strides in social and political development, our great strength, like that of the dinosaur, will find itself incapable of proper control, and men, like the dinosaur, will vanish from the face of the earth."

Great technology and even great art can be produced by men who are not morally adequate. Advanced social and political ideas can be traced on paper by men who are not morally adequate. (The Declaration of Independence was written by slave owners. The Popes have been preaching the principle of subsidiarity for years, but when have they practiced it?)

We have learned to manipulate physical reality and the result has been miraculous technological development. This, then, is our dilemma: we have not yet learned to stimulate spiritual and moral growth. In the so-called spiritual and moral areas we are still primitive, if not barbaric. The civilization that has imagined the existence of, discovered the reality of, and finally used the atom; the civilization which is rapidly developing the science of genetics; the civilization which, given the economic resources, is convinced that it can cure any physical ailment—this same civilization in the area of the human mind works almost on the level of primitive medicine men. And cures are seldom even contemplated. Our educational systems sporadically succeed in spite of themselves. Our gurus and spiritual directors have such limited tools at their disposal.

In establishing adequate conduct, the Church and society at large still depend on legal regimentation and preaching (that is, telling people what to do). Since both are enforcements from the outside, they are doomed to failure in the face of urgent human freedom.

How then are we to narrow the gap between our moral potential and our technological capability? If we are to stimulate our human selves at our very core to new stages of development, we must develop a spiritual technology as advanced as that by which we determine the development of the physical world. The techniques must not destroy nor inhibit human freedom, but must be used in accordance with that freedom. I believe that the rudiments of this technology are things we already know: experience and reflection.

The human experience of each man and of entire communities must be broadened. Narrow experience is one of the primary reasons for prejudice and retrogressive moral reflexes. One way to broaden that experience is through the performing arts, especially drama. I am sure, too, that the sciences will have a great deal to contribute in this regard.

But experience alone is insufficient. Mankind makes no advances by continually judging new experiences merely in the light of past prejudices. With the help of the psychological and social sciences we must discover the techniques by which we can insure that more objective and more thorough reflection will follow the broadened experience.

You see, the idea itself is not revolutionary. We have always known that experience and reflection were the bases of human moral growth; but our educational institutions and our churches and our governments—in short, we ourselves—have found it easier to remain at the warrior stage in human relations, to force one another to act—when necessary—by violence.

The time for admiring the museum-enshrined ideals of the prophets has passed. Now we must take practical steps to make those ideals possible. For with our technology, we warriors have made it physically impossible for any but the meek to possess the earth.

If we look forward to a righteous society where violence is no longer considered necessary, where the ideal of love is the Norm of human conduct, then we must take bold, imaginative steps now to make it possible for violent mankind to change its ways. We must disenthrall ourselves of the superstitious notion that this is an impossible task or that only years of evolutionary process will produce superior thinking men. **We do not have that long.**

Teilhard de Chardin has dreamed that someday, after having harnessed the winds, and the waves, and the other forces of nature, man will direct his attention within himself and harness the power of love; and in so doing, he will have—for the second time in history—discovered fire. I feel, however, that Teilhard's time-table needs to be reversed. Unless man discovers the power of love and learns to harness its energy, he shall be morally unfit to hold the reins that govern the other forces of nature. I feel moreover that man must seek to master the moral forces of nature as systematically as he seeks to dominate the physical forces of nature. Man has become capable of—and is therefore responsible for—his own moral development. His evolution is no longer a matter of merely responding to the forces that surround him; he is not only to dominate the forces outside of himself, but also those within himself. From this point on, the direction of man's evolution is his own responsibility.

(Delivered at a memorial service for Dr. Martin Luther King, Jr.
The Catholic University of America   April 5, 1970)

"Rejoice heart and soul, daughter of Zion!
Shout with gladness, daughter of Jerusalem!
See now, your king comes to you;
he is victorious, he is triumphant,
humble and riding on a donkey,
on a colt, the foal of a donkey.
He will banish chariots from Ephraim
and horses from Jerusalem;
the bow of war will be banished.
He will proclaim peace for the nations.
His empire shall stretch from sea to sea,
from the River to the ends of the earth."

Zechariah 9:9-10

Burk Uzzle

"In a little while
the aggressive man will be no more;
though you search thoroughly,
you will not find him;
but the meek shall possess the earth
to enjoy it in untroubled peace.

Constantine Manos